Stamford

on old picture post

Andrew Jenkins

Bull Running, Stamford

1. Bull Running. Stamford and Tutbury in Staffordshire were the only two British towns known to have practised the "sport" of bull-running where a loose and enraged bull was chased through the streets. This custom, similar to the well-known event in Pamplona in Spain, was first recorded in the 13th century and traditionally took place on 13th November, the anniversary of the massacre of the Danes by Ethelred II in 1002. The custom ended in 1839 amid complaints of its followers being "savage and uncivilised." The Valentine series postcard sent in 1907 depicts a painting made by Mr Everard around 1800 showing the scene in Broad Street.

£3.50

Introduction

Sir Walter Scott described Stamford as the finest sight on the road between London and Edinburgh. Certainly it is a gem of a town, its buildings of mellow limestone giving it an air of quiet gentility. By good fortune, the 18th century townscape has remained largely intact and this was recognised in 1967 when the town centre became the first conservation area in the country.

Stamford is situated in the valley of the River Welland between the edge of the Fens and the uplands of Leicestershire and Rutland. Ermine Street crosses the river here, giving the town its name, from "stone ford," though there was no Roman settlement. The earliest inhabitation was in the 9th century by the Saxons. The Danes also established a borough here and the town grew in importance as a trading and administrative centre. Shortly after the Battle of Hastings, William the Conqueror built a castle at Stamford and the town prospered. In the 12th century there were fourteen churches, two monasteries and grand stone-built houses. Wool and grain provided the wealth, and a local cloth called haberget was exported all over Europe. However, this prosperity was not to last, and a downturn in the wool trade brought decline in the 15th and 16th centuries. Around this time William Cecil, a local man, rose to become Queen Elizabeth 1st's most trusted councillor. His immense wealth funded the building of Burghley House and enabled his control of much of the town. From this time the interests of the Cecils and Stamford were closely linked. The town began to grow in importance again, a canal was built linking it to the ports on The Wash and the coaching trade on The Great North Road brought prosperity. The Cecils (Marquesses of Exeter from 1801) initiated several redevelopment schemes in the 18th century.

By the 19th century Stamford was growing fast, but a lack of enthusiasm by the Marquess for the proposed London to York railway led to the line being routed through Peterborough, sparing Stamford industrialisation and preserving its older buildings. This was not the only time that events have helped preserve the town. In 1939 World War Two stopped construction of a damaging relief road through the town centre. Ironically, its preservation holds the key to the town's future. Stamford is now a popular tourist destination as well as a pleasant place to live and work.

The postcards in this book return us to the early 20th century when Stamford was a market and manufacturing town. One hundred years ago, in a world without telephones or television, postcards were the equivalent of today's e-mail or home video. At a time when illustrations in the press were limited, they were an ideal way to send a pictorial message quickly. In the years up to World War One, postcard sending became an international craze and they depicted every conceivable subject. Each town or village had at least one postcard publisher. In Stamford there were at least a dozen publishers of which Dolby Bros. were prominent in quality and coverage. After 1918, postcard use declined and these 'time capsules' remained buried in attics and drawers. Now rediscovered by collectors, they enable us to rediscover a lost world.

Andrew Jenkins
June 2002

All postcards from the author's collection.

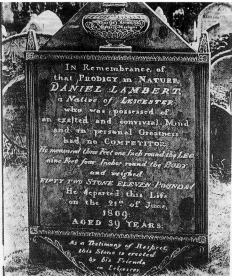

2. Daniel Lambert weighed in at 53 stone and measured 9ft 4in around the waist when he died in Stamford in 1809. He was born in Leicester in 1770 and was formerly keeper of the Bridewell Prison there. When this closed, he reluctantly decided to exhibit himself as a curiosity and travelled the country, arriving in Stamford in June 1809 during the horse races which were held on Wittering Heath. He died suddenly in the "Waggon & Horses Inn" and is buried in St. Martin's churchyard, where it is said twenty men were needed to lower the coffin into the grave.

S.F.S. SERIES   STAMFORD, FROM THE AIR   10839

3. An aerial view looking south-east over Stamford taken in the 1920s with All Saints church in the centre. The curving course of the medieval town wall can be seen on the left, traced by North Street and West Street. The River Welland and Meadows are to the right, with the edge of Burghley Park just appearing top right. Postcard published by Surrey Flying Services.

4. No book on Stamford can fail to mention **Burghley House** or its owners, the Cecil family. The house was built for William Cecil, the first Lord Burghley (1520-1598), Lord High Treasurer to Queen Elizabeth I. His descendants were created Earls of Exeter in 1605 and Marquesses in 1801. The mansion about which Defoe said *"It looks more like a town than a house"* sits in a park designed by Capability Brown extending to the edge of the town. Postcard by Dolby Bros. c. 1912.

5. William Cecil (1876-1956), the 5th **Marquess of Exeter,** is seen here with the hounds of the Fitzwilliam Hunt in the stable yard of Burghley House. He presided over a period when the family faced financial difficulties and were forced to sell off large parts of their estates. In 1909 he was elected Town Mayor. Postcard published by G.F. Hinson and posted in 1909.

S 2072 16 Aug. 1910   GIRLS HIGH SCHOOL, ST. MARTINS, STAMFORD.

6. A string of horses are being led down **High Street, St. Martin's,** towards St. Martin's Church and the Town Bridge. The building on the right is the High School for Girls and beyond is the "Bull and Swan Inn." Postcard published by W.H. Smith in 1910.

Gymnasium Girls High School Stamford.

7. The **Girls High School** was opened in 1877. This physical education class in the gas-lit gymnasium would be considered rather overdressed by today's standards. Postcard published by Mrs Nichols.

8. Children and teachers gather round the maypole in the cramped yard of **St. Martin's School** to celebrate Empire Day. The school was on the corner of Kettering Road and High Street, St. Martin's. Notice the blackboard in the corner which lists songs such as *"The British Grenadiers," "Red White and Blue,"* and the *"National Anthem."* The group of mothers peering through holes in the fence adds an amusing touch. Anonymous photographer 1908.

9. The postcard photographer Dolby took a series of views from the top of the tower of **St. Martin's Church.** This card looks directly north-west over the town centre. From left to right the towers of All Saints, St. John's, St. Mary's and St. Michael's churches are prominent. The fields in the background have all now been covered by later housing developments. The scaffolding on St. Mary's dates the picture to 1913.

10. Known as *"one of the greatest inns in England"*, **The "George Hotel"** dates back to the 16th century. It was rebuilt in its present form with the famous gallows sign over the road in 1724. The sign on the left is outside the works of the firm of Pick who built motor cars in the town between 1899 and 1924. Dolby Bros. postcard c. 1912.

11. It's hard to believe that this was the route of the Great North Road (A1) when this peaceful view over the **Town Bridge** to St. Mary's church was taken. The present bridge shown here opened in 1849 and was partly funded by the Midland Railway. It replaced an earlier structure built in the 12th century. Postcard published by Dolby Bros. c. 1910.

12. The Marquess of Exeter was Mayor of Stamford from 1909. Here he reads the Proclamation of King George V in May 1910 standing on the steps of the **Town Hall.** It was built in the 1770s but the west entrance and steps were remodelled in 1951. Postcard by G.F. Hinson.

13. Another postcard showing the Marquess of Exeter in his role as Mayor. This time he is in full regalia heading the Mayors' Sunday procession over the **Town Bridge** on a bleak November day in 1909. Postcard photographed by Mrs Nichols.

14. During World War 1 large numbers of troops passed through the town before leaving for the trenches in France. A soldier of the 6th Essex Regiment billeted in Tenter Lane sent this card in 1915 saying, *"This is our brass band and Battalion going to church last Sunday. We are good? boys."* The view is looking down **St. Mary's Hill** and shows the long-closed "Queen's Head Inn" and Bunning's Temperance Hotel (now Stamford Music Shop).

15. In this postcard of around 1910 an express to Peterborough is drawing into the **Midland Railway Station**. The line from Leicester to Peterborough was the first to reach the town in 1846. Building the line was difficult because the promoters had to face opposition from both the Marquess of Exeter and Lord Harborough of Stapleford Park, near Melton Mowbray. Later a branch line of the London & North Western Railway connected this station to Market Harborough.

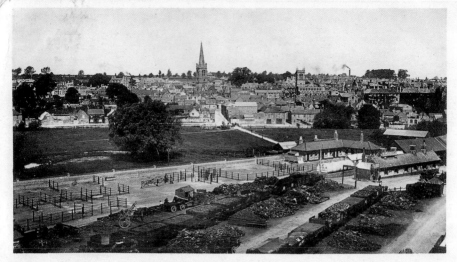

S 9201   BIRD'S EYE VIEW OF STAMFORD.

16. The Midland Station possessed an extensive goods yard including a five-storey grain warehouse. The photographer has climbed to the top to get this view over the goods yard and cattle market to the Meadows and town beyond. Notice the busy coal trade at a time when this fuel was the only form of heating. The warehouse was demolished in 1968 and the goods yard is now a housing development. W. H. Smith series postcard, sent in 1912.

STAMFORD GNR.

17. Partly as a result of criticism that his lack of support led to the building of the London to York railway through Peterborough instead of Stamford, the Marquess of Exeter promoted the building of a branch line to Essendine where it met the Great Northern Railway. **Water Street Station** opened in 1856. Another line was built in 1867 to Wansford on the Peterborough to Northampton line, and both branch trains are seen here on a card by G.F. Hinson c. 1906. These passenger services were never economic and both had ended by 1959.

18. After leaving Water Street Station the branch railway to Essendine crossed the river near **Hudd's Mill** on a rather flimsy iron girder bridge supported by timber piles. This group of workmen was probably responsible for its upkeep. The railway closed completely in 1969 and the bridge and its embankments were cleared away and a pumping station built on part of the site.

COPYRIGHT.
SMD. 4
TOWN FROM MEADOWS. STAMFORD.
LILYWHITE LTD.
TRIANGLE HALIFAX

19. An unusually busy scene on **The Meadows** in the 1930s. This area of water-meadows in the middle of the town is still partially used for cattle grazing and is a notable feature of Stamford. The Roman Ermine Street crossed the river Welland not far from this point. Postcard by Lilywhite of Halifax, posted 1942.

A Great Flood at Stamford

20. The Meadows area has always been prone to flooding as this picture shows. Notable floods occurred in 1880 and 1897 when houses were flooded up to 6ft deep. This picture is believed to date from around 1900. Despite the building of new defences serious floods still occur occasionally in the town. Postcard published by George W. Wilson, posted in 1912.

SPA & WEIR STAMFORD MEADOWS

21. Situated at the far western end of the Meadows near the A1 by-pass, an **Ironwater Spa** was discovered in 1819. and renovated in 1864 by the Mayor, John Paradise. It later fell into disrepair, but the monument was restored a few years ago. Dolby Bros. postcard c. 1912.

22. The Stamford Hotel. This impressive building was built around 1810 on the site of a medieval inn, the "Black Bull." The financier of the project was Sir Gerard Noel of Exton Hall in Rutland. He was a Whig and it said that it was built as a snub against the Tory Cecils who controlled the political life of the town. The building is now part of the Stamford Walk shopping arcade. Postcard published by Dolby Bros. and posted in 1911.

23. St. Mary's Street, looking west from the top of St. Mary's Hill. The ninth Earl of Exeter built the range of shops on the right in the late 18th century. On the left, the corner building was part of a project started by Richard Newcomb; the *Stamford Mercury* proprietor in 1843, to create a grand street of shops connecting to the High Street. Newcomb died in 1851 and his vision was never completed. Postcard posted in 1905, publisher unknown.

24. St. Mary's Vaults. This inn to the east of "The Stamford Hotel" dates from the Middle Ages and in the 18th century was known as "The Eagle and Child." It is seen here before the plastering was removed from the building, revealing half-timbering beneath. Postcard by unknown publisher sent in 1920.

25. Red Lion Square has been the site of a market since the days of the Danish settlement in Stamford. To the left of St. John's church, the buildings with ornate signwriting date from the 15th century and may once have been a Guildhall. The unusual roof lantern was added around 1830 and had seats inside. Dawson's jewellers now occupy the shop. Valentine series postcard c.1908.

40691   MARKET SQUARE AND ST. JOHN'S CHURCH, STAMFORD   VALENTINES SERIES

26. This photograph is thought to depict troops of the Lincolnshire Volunteer Regiment on parade in **Red Lion Square** after returning from the Boer War in 1904. Part of the 18th century shop front in the background was replaced by a brick building in the 1930s. Postcard by G.F. Hinson.

27. Barn Hill. This street running into All Saints Place has had a number of different names over the centuries. It has always been the site of prosperous housing. The gates to the right belong to Barn Hill House which in the 19th century was home of the millionaire, Edward Brown. The spires of All Saints and St. Mary's churches are in the background. Dolby Bros. postcard, posted in 1913.

KING CHARLES GATEWAY, STAMFORD

28. The gateway, once a postern gate in the town walls, stands in the garden of **No 9 Barn Hill** backing onto North Street. In the early 1700s the house was owned by the eccentric William Stukeley, an antiquarian and early archaeologist. It was he who rebuilt the gate and postulated the unproven story that Charles 1 passed through the gate in May 1646 whilst evading Cromwells' soldiers and shortly before his capitulation at Southwell, Notts. Postcard published by E.F. Rogers (successor to J.E.C. Potter), and posted in 1908.

29. The narrow **Red Lion Street** connects Broad Street to Red Lion Square. Some of the old shops on the left were rebuilt in the 1940s. The sign of the "Lord Nelson" pub can be seen to the right. This closed in 1961 and used to have a wooden statue of Bacchus over the door. Dolby Bros. postcard used in 1921.

S 9203   BROWNE'S HOSPITAL, STAMFORD.

30. The **Browne's Hospital** almshouses were founded by William Browne, a wealthy wool merchant in the 15th century and were rebuilt in 1870. On the right are the offices of Blackstone & Co, engineers. They were replaced in 1913 by a new building which was later to become the Central Cinema. W.H. Smith series postcard, posted in 1915.

31. Browne's Hospital. William Browne endowed the hospital to house ten poor men looked after by a staff of a warden and two women. Eight of the inhabitants are seen here wearing top hats and breeches, together with a nurse or matron. The picture was taken in the courtyard at the rear of the building. Postcard c. 1905 by unknown publisher.

BROAD STREET. SHOW

32. Broad Street has traditionally been the site of Stamf
until 1887 and the Friday Market and Mid Lent Fair are :
appear to be selling what would now be classed as anti
by E.F. Rogers (successor to J.E.C. Potter) and posted in

G MARKET. STAMFORD.

main market since medieval times. A cattle market was based here
held here. In this picture, dating from around 1900, the stall-holders
but which were then general household goods. Postcard published
8.

33. In 1913 Blackstone & Co opened a large new showroom on the site of their earlier offices. By 1925 it had been sold to The Cambridge Cinema Co and reopened as the **"Central Cinema."** It is seen here in 1929 when a film called *"The Isle of Lost Ships"* was showing. Disaster struck the cinema in 1937 when it burnt down. Its replacement was built in typical art deco cinema style and survives as a night club. Postcard by Jerome Ltd.

34. A busy scene at the western end of the **High Street** looking towards Freeman, Hardy & Willis' shoe shop on Red Lion Square. Notice the figure of an eagle on the parapet. This was removed in the First World War because of anti-German sentiments. Postcard publisher unknown c. 1908.

THE HIGH STREET, STAMFORD

35. This view of the south side of the **High Street** shows the premises of two prominent local postcard publishers. The card was published by J.E.C. Potter, whose shop is far left next to the unusually named "Pineapple Inn." Next to this is the projecting bay of a 16th century building which was dismantled and taken to York Castle Museum when the present Woolworths' store was built in 1936. Further along, the shop with the large signboard under the tower of St. John's church is Dolby Bros., probably the best-known photographer and postcard publisher in the area. Postcard used in 1908.

36. A quiet view looking up **Ironmonger Street** towards Broad Street, photographed from the High Street end. Dickinson's Cycle Works half way up the right hand side occupies the last remaining part of the "Blue Bell," a large 16th century inn which formerly took up the entire east side of this street. Dolby Bros. postcard c. 1912.

37. A crowd await the announcement of the January 1906 General Election resu
Stamford was in the Kesteven constituency and results were counted at Bourn
The news was sometimes greeted by stone-throwing and window-breakin
at the beginning of the 18th century and is the oldest newspaper continua

itside the *Stamford Mercury* office formerly at **No 62 High Street**.
ese were then telegrammed to the *Mercury* office for proclamation.
nce the several policemen on duty. The *Stamford Mercury* was founded
blished under the same title. Postcard by G.F. Hinson.

38. The east end of **High Street** near the entrance to Maiden Lane. Prominent on the left is the Public Library which was rebuilt from the open portico of The Shambles or market in 1906. A Great Northern Railway delivery cart from Water Street Station stands on the right. In the background in front of the Co-op is a horse drawn water bowser used for street cleaning. Dolby Bros. Postcard sent in 1910.

Co-operative Stores, High Street, Stamford. Opened Feb. 12th, 1910.

39. This postcard was issued to commemorate the opening of the new **Peterborough Co-operative Store** in 1910. The opening ceremony drew a large crowd; speeches were made and the Town Band played. Afterwards there was a public tea in the Assembly Rooms for 700 people. In 1966 the building was extended to the right.

40. The buildings nearest the camera on both sides of **Maiden Lane** have now been demolished. The 16th century house on the right was pulled down in 1904, dating this picture to before that time. In other respects this view is still recognisable today, though the pavements are now narrower. Postcard publisher unknown.

41. Remarkably this is now the staircase inside **Walker's Bookstore** in the High Street. The passage that ran to the west of the building was incorporated into the store in the 1960s and the outside of the former 16th century jettied timber-framed house can still be seen at first floor level. Anonymously-published postcard c. 1904.

Stamford.

Dear Arnold,
I think you collect picture "coast-guards" so here is one to add to the collection. I hope you are all well & flourishing. I'm well where I am staying is such a pretty little place, about 1½ miles from Stamford.

Love to all. 24.7.02. *November Sheep Fair.* Your affectionate cousin Long Winnie.

42. St. Peters' Hill gridlocked with sheep during the November Sheep Market. This was traditionally held during the Fair of Saints Simon and Jude on 8th and 9th of the month when there were also markets for horses, cheese and vegetables held in the town. The view is looking east past St. Peter's Callis to the appropriately named Sheepmarket. Wrench series postcard posted in July 1902.

43. The narrow **Castle Street** has been considerably altered. In 1939 the buildings on the left were removed to make way for a link to a town relief road that would have run across the Meadows. Thankfully this was never built. Three pubs are shown here; The "Castle" on the right and "The Prince of Wales" on the left have long closed. The rear of the old "London Inn" is behind. This has also now been rebuilt. Dolby Bros. postcard sent in 1932.

BLUECOATS SCHOOL STAMFORD. 834.

44. **Bluecoat School** was founded in 1704 as a charity school by the town magistrates. Its name is derived from the colour of the boys' uniform and was originally situated in St. Paul's Street. In 1838 this new school building was opened on St. Peter's Hill and is now a Masonic Centre. Dolby Bros. postcard posted in 1915.

ST PETERS ST STAMFORD. 834.

45. Looking eastward along **St. Peter's Street** towards the town centre. On the left is the Territorial Drill Hall, opened in 1913 shortly before this photograph was taken. The signs of the now closed "Chequers Inn," left and "The Greyhound" (now "St. Peter's Inn") can also be seen. Dolby Bros. postcard.

46. A view taken from roughly the same spot looking westwards along **St. Peter's Street**. However, this photograph was taken before the building of the Drill Hall and shows the wall of Blackstone's original Rutland Iron Works on the left. The building projecting into the road is Hopkins Hospital, an almshouse built in 1770 after the demolition of St. Peters Gate. Postcard sent in 1908, publisher unknown.

47. Rutland Terrace. This terrace of distinctive three-storey town houses was built in 1829 and commands an uninterrupted view over the Welland valley. St. Peter's Street and Hopkins Hospital are in the background. Unknown postcard publisher.

48. The sender of this postcard refers to these rather grand houses that had just been built in 1907 on **Tinwell Road**. She goes on to say: *"Stamford does seem rotten after Manchester & Liverpool, I can't seem to settle a bit."* The photograph is taken near the junction with Roman Bank, so named because it follows the course of Ermine Street. Postcard published by Mrs Nichols and sent in 1907.

49. The houses on **Queens Walk** off West Street were newly-built when this picture was taken. The unmade road looks deceptively wide, but today with pavements and parked cars it is quite a narrow street. New housing estates have replaced the trees in the background. Dolby Bros. postcard sent in 1918.

PHOTO. OF HAYES & SON'S SHOWROOMS, STAMFORD, LINCS.

50. This advertising card for Hayes & Son Carriage Works in **Scotgate** was used to promote their exhibit of dairy vehicles at the London Dairy Show in 1922. The firm was founded in the 1820s and grew to become internationally-known as makers of horse-drawn vehicles. The large factory and showroom on Scotgate was damaged by fire in 1921 and finally closed in 1924. The site is now a car park.

S 9213   SCOTGATE. STAMFORD.

51. Scotgate was the northern entrance of the Great North Road into the town and was lined with numerous small inns. The view is looking towards the town centre with the spires of All Saints and St. Mary's churches in the background. Wheatley's Garage on the left is displaying an interesting range of enamel signs. W.H. Smith & Sons postcard c. 1908.

52. This is the northern end of Scotgate with Empingham Road leading off to the left. The imposing **Rock Terrace**, left and Clock House, centre, were built by Richard Newcomb, the proprietor of the *Stamford Mercury*, in the 1840s. His villa, Rock House, was behind the trees to the left and is now a retirement home. The postcard, published by C.H. Haynes, dates from the 1920s. It was sent by an American soldier billeted here in World War Two. The message refers to the baseball games played on land behind Rock Terrace.

53. **St. Paul's Street** is a very early street running east from the old Danish settlement and contains several medieval houses. In the centre of the picture, a shepherd and his dog are driving sheep round the corner into Star Lane outside the old "Half Moon Inn," which was rebuilt in 1938. The cottages to the left were also removed to make way for a car showroom. Postcard c. 1905, publisher unknown.

St Leonard's St Stamford. 839

54. St. Leonard's Street was originally known as Cornstall, the site of a corn market. This was a centre of the bull-running custom, the ends of the street being blocked off and a bull turned loose. The "Olive Branch" pub on the left was the headquarters of the bullards or bull-chasers, and the bull itself was kept in a yard further down the street. Dolby Bros. postcard c. 1912.

55. On 9th September 1909 workmen discovered a leaden coffin containing a mummified body near the site of the Blackfriars friary off **Wharf Road.** The corpse was thought to be that of John of Stamford, a monk who died around 1348. The remains of "Friar John," as he became known, were given full burial rites in the Stamford Cemetery and a series of postcards by G.F. Hinson recorded the event.

Leaden Coffin found at Stamford 9-9-09

56. The **Infirmary Gateway** at the junction of St. Paul's Street and Ryhall Road. This gateway is the last remnant of the Franciscan Grey Friary, and although much-altered, dates from the 14th century. The friary itself was apparently an impressive building with a beautiful church and spire. The mother of Richard II was said to have been buried there in a *"sumptuous chapel."* Dolby Bros. postcard sent in 1915.

57. The Union Workhouse was built on **Ryhall Road** in 1902 and replaced an earlier workhouse on Barnack Road. The new building could accommodate 175 poor and needy people in several blocks, and tramps were allowed to stay in wards near the gates. In the 1940s it became St. George's Home and part of the National Health Service. However, even recently, elderly people hated the prospect of going to *"the workhouse!"* The home has now been pulled down and houses erected on the site. Dolby Bros. postcard c. 1910.

58. Recreation Ground. A busy summer afternoon scene on "The Rec" with a bowls match in progress behind the tennis court. In the 19th century the North Fields were enclosed; terraced housing and this recreation ground were built on the old open fields. Dolby Bros. postcard, posted in 1914.

59. This long row of terraced houses was built around 1905 for workers in the engineering works along **Ryhall Road**. Notice the delivery boy and the state of the road, now busy with traffic to Bourne. Postcard sent in 1906, unknown publisher.

60. Blackstone & Co were once Stamford's largest employer and were known worldwide for their oil engines and agricultural implements. The firm started in 1837 in the Sheep Market and later moved to St. Peter's Street. However, expansion required a new factory and this on Ryhall Road was opened in 1887 with a direct rail link. Sadly, in recent years the business declined and final closure has recently been announced. Dolby Bros. postcard c. 1912.

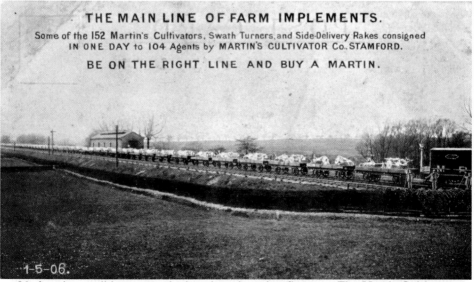

THE MAIN LINE OF FARM IMPLEMENTS.

Some of the 152 Martin's Cultivators, Swath Turners, and Side-Delivery Rakes consigned IN ONE DAY to 104 Agents by MARTIN'S CULTIVATOR Co., STAMFORD.

BE ON THE RIGHT LINE AND BUY A MARTIN.

61. Another well-known agricultural engineering firm was **The Martin Cultivator Co.** This was founded in 1902 and opened a factory on Ryhall Road in 1907. Their works were also served by a rail siding. This view of an extremely long train load of farm implements is believed to have been taken just west of the Midland Station in Stamford in 1906.

62. Grocer's Cart. A reminder of a time when groceries were delivered to your front door. This is the delivery cart of Edward Young of 12-13 St. John's St. with its driver Jack Wade and his wife. It was stabled at Young's warehouse in Castle Dyke, and Mr Wade lived in a tied cottage nearby. His round originally included the local villages but, around 1910, horse power was relegated to town deliveries by the arrival of a Model T Ford van.

63. The builders, **Bowman & Sons,** are still known nationally as specialist restorers of stone buildings and churches. This postcard sent in 1910 shows their workshops in Cherryhold Road. A fascinating array of intricately-carved church furniture is being made, including a font cover and several screens.